7 Stoic Principles You Must Know

Wisdom for Confidence and Calm, Building Inner Strength, Finding Inner Peace and Living a Resilient Life.

By Gregory Atticus

Table of Contents

- Embracing the Transience of Existence
  - Incorporating Reflection into Daily Practices

5. Practice Gratitude and Contentment
   - The Power of Gratitude in Stoicism
   - Finding Contentment Amidst Life's Challenges

6. Live by Nature
   - Understanding the Natural Order
   - Applying Stoic Principles to Align with Nature

7. Cultivate Inner Strength and Resilience
   - Build Mental Fortitude
   - Strategies for Navigating Adversity with Composure

Conclusion
   - Summarizing the 7 Principles
   - Encouraging Continued Practice and Growth

Introduction

Overview of Stoicism

Have you ever felt like life is tossing challenges your way, and you're urgently attempting to bat them away? I got it. We're all in this together, navigating the mess that is existence. What if I told you there's a mindset that may convert those curveballs into chances for growth?

That's where Stoicism comes in.

Stoicism isn't simply a jargon; it's a meaningful method of addressing life. It's about accepting that although we can't control everything that occurs to us, we can influence how we respond. Picture it as a timeless handbook to tackling life with elegance, courage, and an unchanging sense of self.

Welcome to a journey of self-discovery and perseverance. I'm pleased to be your guide into the fascinating realm of Stoicism, a philosophy that's been a compass for many throughout history, including Marcus Aurelius and Seneca. Being a Stoic doesn't imply repressing emotions or maintaining a stoic look; it's about finding calm in turmoil and wisdom in the face of uncertainty.

In this examination, we'll break down the wisdom of the Stoics into seven principles, each meant to strengthen you in the face of life's uncertainties. From concentrating on what's under your control to seeing challenges as stepping stones, we'll dig into practical tactics and timeless thoughts.

Get a seat, open your mind, and let's go on a journey to implement these Stoic concepts in the following year. Trust me; you will discover a new approach to life.

Relevance of Stoic Philosophy Today

Ever found yourself drowning in the craziness of our fast-paced, ever-shifting world? I hear you. In a culture that bombards us with noise and unanticipated difficulties, the wisdom of the Stoics has never been more applicable.

Let's be honest - life throws curveballs, and Stoicism isn't about repressing feelings or adopting a hard mask. It's about navigating the storm with a calm core, finding strength in adversity, and, most importantly, realizing that the only thing we control is our reaction to what occurs.

Think of Stoicism as your hidden weapon, your guidance to fighting the current turmoils with a calm mind. As we handle the pressures of jobs, relationships, and the unexpected, Stoic philosophy gives us a path for living. It's about building a mentality that enables us to cope with life's uncertainties rather than getting carried away.

This isn't about dusty old beliefs; it's about restoring your sanity, finding resilience, and achieving a deep feeling of serenity amid today's turmoil. Are you ready to tow this move with me?

Walk with me.

Focus on What You Can Control

We must concentrate the majority of our time and mental energy entirely on what is within our ability to manage or directly impact.

As Marcus Aurelius said,

"Today I escaped anxiety. Or no, I disregarded it because it was inside me, in my perceptions—not outside."

He realized it was foolish to expend effort worrying about external things like gossip, petty critiques, fleeting fortunes or other people's business that we cannot govern. By directing energy exclusively into meaningful activity that coincides with our values and objectives, we establish the mentality and habits essential for self-discipline.

- Understanding the Area of Control

Focusing exclusively on what I can control has been a game-changer for

I know it seems easier said than done, right? Life has this habit of throwing twists our way, and suddenly, we're juggling a dozen things at once.

Here's the secret weapon; Understanding the Area of Control.

Picture this area as your particular domain of influence. It's where your activities, choices, and energies genuinely matter. Beyond this area? Well, there's the domain of the uncontrolled, the unexpected, the stuff that can drive us insane if we let it. Trust me; I've been there.

It's not about creating barriers or avoiding obstacles; it's about being deliberate with where you put your mental and emotional energy. When you comprehend this notion, you are not just going through life; you are traveling with purpose.

- Practical Techniques for Shifting Focus

Now, I'm no superhero, but I've picked up some useful tactics for shifting focus in mayhem. They are:

✓ First up, the "Pause and Assess" technique. It's about taking that split second to breathe and examine the circumstance. Trust me, it works wonderfully.

✓ Then, there's the "Mindful Redirect." When you notice your thoughts going to the uncontrolled things, gently lead them back to your sphere. It's like a mental GPS recalibrating your concentration.

✓ Lastly, the "One Step at a Time" method. Life's not a sprint; it's a marathon. Break down large tasks into bite-sized steps. It's remarkable how empowered it feels to tick off those tiny chores.

Curb Destructive Emotions Through Logic

-The Stoic Approach to Emotions

Marcus Aurelius advised aHyout the hazards of harmful emotions like wrath, bitterness, worry, or sadness overcoming our rational control centers if left uncontrolled.

He wrote,

"Passions paralyze. Only action based on clear understanding gives you back control."

As a Stoic and diligent journal writer, Marcus Aurelius suggested employing written logical exercises to offset these exhausting feelings.

For instance, if he battled with rage when upset, he advised asking questions like:

• How significant is this?

• What good would come from staying angry?

He recommended looking at the bigger picture objectively before responding.

- Implementing Rational Thinking in Daily Life

This isn't about being an emotionless robot; it is about being in charge of your emotions.

So, let us get practical. Here are five techniques I have learned to pepper a touch of sensible thinking into our everyday lives.

✓ First up, the "Pause and Breathe" motion. It seems easy, but believe me, a deep breath can be a game-changer when emotions are churning.

✓ Then there is the "Journaling" when we wrestle those feelings onto paper, giving them a one-two punch of reasoning.

✓ Ever tried the "Perspective Shift"?
It's about viewing things from a new viewpoint, and it's surprisingly effective.

✓ "Mindful Moments" is all about living in the now, enjoying the present rather than getting carried away by emotions.

✓ Lastly, the "Logic Check" — a short reality check to verify whether our feelings fit with what's actually going on.

View Obstacles as Opportunities

The Stoics preached willingly enduring inevitable discomfort or hardship without pointless complaint or self-pity as a powerful pathway to self-mastery.

As Marcus Aurelius wrote:

"The ideal person exercises self-control in the face of troubles he meets...and willingly does the things a rational self-respecting social being would do."

Part of self-respect, after all, means honoring commitments even when inconvenient. No one respects those who shirk duty when challenges arise.

He further adds,

"Don't hope that events will turn out the way you want; welcome events in whichever way they happen: this is the path to peace."

- Transforming Challenges into Growth

View obstacles not as roadblocks, but as opportunities for growth.

Here's the trick for transforming challenges into growth. Think of it like a sculptor chiseling a masterpiece from a block of marble. Each obstacle you face is a chance to carve out a stronger, wiser version of yourself.

How do we do this? Well, it starts with reframing. Instead of seeing problems, we see puzzles waiting to be solved. Then there's the power of perspective—taking a step back to see the bigger picture. It's amazing how obstacles shrink when you view them from a distance.

And let's not forget about resilience—the muscle you flex when facing adversity. It's about bouncing back, learning, and evolving. Together, let's explore how to not just navigate challenges but to thrive in the midst of them. Ready to turn stumbling blocks into stepping stones? Join me in uncovering the art of transforming obstacles into opportunities for growth. Let's grow through what we go through.

- Strategies for Changing Perspectives.

Let's dive deeper into the art of viewing obstacles as opportunities by exploring strategies for changing perspectives.

✓ First off, there's the "Zoom Out" technique. When faced with a challenge, try zooming out mentally. See it in the context of your broader journey. Suddenly, that mountain looks more like a hill, and you realize you've conquered tougher terrain before.

✓ Next up, we have the "Silver Lining Search." It's about actively seeking the positive aspects within a challenge. What lessons can be learned? What new opportunities might emerge? It's like finding treasure in the midst of a storm.

✓ Ever tried the "Empathy Lens"? Imagine how someone else might see your situation.

This not only broadens your perspective but often reveals solutions you hadn't considered.

✓ Then there's the "Future Self Reflection." Picture yourself a year from now, looking back at this challenge. What advice would that future, wiser you give? It's a powerful way to gain insight and navigate the present with clarity.

✓ Lastly, the "Gratitude Pivot." Shift your focus from what's lacking to what you have. Gratitude has this incredible ability to reframe obstacles as opportunities for appreciation.

Reflect Regularly on the Brevity of Life

Marcus Aurelius famously started each day, observing, "I could lose everything today." He fully believed in the significance of intentionally pondering on death and understanding the fleeting nature of all things, including life itself, as a means to enjoying this present and activating self-discipline.

Memento mori, meaning "Remember you must die" in Latin, was crucial to his worldview.

To paraphrase Marcus explicitly on this phenomenon: "Think of yourself as dead. You have spent your life. Now take what's left and enjoy it properly."

What bigger motive could there be?

- Embracing the Transience of Existence

It seems heavy, I know, but stick with me because this Stoic idea is a game-changer. Life is this wonderful, transitory dance, and sometimes we fail to truly immerse ourselves in the music.

Embracing the impermanence of life isn't about getting lost in philosophical thinking; it's about infusing every moment with purpose. Picture it as adding bright brushstrokes to the canvas of your life narrative. When we understand the limited nature of our time, suddenly, the banal becomes exceptional.

I've discovered that taking time to halt, breathe, and think about the fragility of life has this amazing capacity to prioritize what is essential. It's not a morbid activity; it's a celebration of the moment. It's about constructing a life that corresponds with our innermost beliefs and interests.

Reflecting periodically on the shortness of life isn't a call to haste but an encouragement to cherish. Let's make every pulse count.

-Incorporating Reflection into Daily Practices

Now that we've touched on the important notion of appreciating life's impermanence, let's discuss how we might weave reflection into our everyday lives.

Think of it as adding a sprinkling of awareness to your routine — a slight push to enjoy the small moments and learn from the trip.

Incorporating introspection into your everyday activities doesn't have to be a large, time-consuming event. It's about finding those pockets of peace among the busyness. Maybe it's a peaceful cup of coffee in the morning or a quick break before sleep.

Consider it your daily encounter with yourself. Reflect on the highs and lows, the laughs, the hardships, and the times that passed by unnoticed. It's not about focusing on the past; it's about gleaning insight into the present and future.

This simple act turns routine into ritual, and each day becomes a canvas for self-discovery.

So, make it a practice to carve out these thoughtful periods. Trust me; the insights obtained are like valuable nuggets that enhance the fabric of our lives.

Practice Gratitude and Contentment

-The Power of Gratitude in Stoicism

Let's unwrap a hidden weapon in the Stoic arsenal: the practice of gratitude and its big boost in establishing a Stoic attitude. In the scurry of our everyday lives, Stoicism challenges us to stop and embrace the transformational power of thankfulness.

Picture thankfulness as the cornerstone of a Stoic attitude — it's not just about politeness or acknowledging benefits; it's a dynamic force that influences how we view and behave in the world. I've come to see that, in the Stoic philosophy, gratitude isn't a simple feeling but a purposeful instrument for fostering resilience and contentment.

In the sphere of Stoicism, cultivating thankfulness is like fine-tuning a mental muscle. It's about teaching ourselves to change emphasis from what's missing to what's present. By noticing and enjoying the present moment, we develop a foundation of satisfaction, liberating ourselves from the endless quest for more.

- Finding Contentment Amidst Life's Challenges

Here are three tried-and-true strategies I've learned to locate that elusive sensation of satisfaction.

✓ First up, it's the "Gratitude Scroll." Take time each day to mentally browse through the things you're thankful for. It's like building a mental scrapbook of delight amid the daily grind, a powerful technique that redirects your emphasis from what's missing to what's available.

✓ Next, let us discuss "Acceptance." Life isn't always a smooth sail, but appreciating the present moment, warts and all, maybe tremendously freeing. It's about admitting the truth of the circumstance without allowing it to take your tranquility.

✓ And then, there's the "Breathe Break." When life's tumult becomes overpowering, press pause. Take a deep breath. It's astonishing how a moment of calm can be a game-changer, providing you the room to discover satisfaction even in the middle of adversity.

Live by Nature

- Understanding the Natural Order

Let's dig into the fundamental notion of living by nature, a basic part of Stoicism. It's not about communicating with words (although that's nice too); it's about aligning our lives with the underlying order of the cosmos. So, what is the stoic scope?

Living by nature in Stoicism is about realizing the vast plain of existence. It's accepting that some things are beyond our control, and seeking to manage them simply leads to frustration. Instead, it is about accepting the ebb and flow, and recognizing the natural sequence of events.

In my path with Stoicism, living by nature has been the compass that steers me across the stormy seas of doubt. It's about adjusting, not resisting.

- Applying Stoic Principles to Align with Nature

Stoicism isn't about fleeing the world; it's about handling it properly. So, how do we cope with the natural order? Here are a few guidelines to consider:

✓ Recognizing the things under control: Stoicism urges us to determine what's within our control and what's not. By concentrating our efforts on what we can control, we align with the natural order, eliminating unneeded upheaval.

✓ Embracing Acceptance: Stoic acceptance is not passive resignation but an active embrace of reality. It's about knowing that life develops in its own manner, and our tranquility resides in accepting it rather than struggling against it.

✓ Cultivating Resilience: Life is a series of unexpected occurrences, and Stoicism teaches us to create resilience. By perceiving problems as chances for progress, we learn to adapt, bounce back, and align ourselves with the ebb and flow of life.

Cultivate Inner Strength and Resilience

-Build Mental Fortitude

Let us dig into a tremendous area — fostering inner strength and resilience, the fundamental basis of a Stoic worldview. Life is no stroll in the park, and I realize that; we all encounter storms, but here is the Stoic secret: cultivating mental fortitude.

Think of it as establishing a mental fortress, a shelter that remains firm throughout life's tumult. It is not about avoiding obstacles but creating the strength to weather them with elegance.

In my own experience, establishing mental fortitude has been transformative. It's like doing repetitions in the mental gym, strengthening the muscles that let us stand strong under adversity. Stoicism encourages us to consider losses not as failures but as chances for character molding.

So, how do you go on this journey? It's about accepting pain, addressing anxieties, and seeing barriers as stepping stones. Together, let's study the practical stages of strengthening mental fortitude in the Stoic tradition. Trust me, it's not about getting invincible; it's about becoming incredibly resilient. Ready to strengthen your intellect and tackle life's obstacles with unshakeable strength? Join me; the trip is as gratifying as the goal.

-Strategies for Navigating Adversity with Composure

Let's have a heart-to-heart on negotiating hardship with calm because, let's be real, life throws curveballs that may leave us feeling like we're in a whirlwind. So, here are a few tried-and-true tactics that I have found to be tremendously useful in retaining calm when the storm strikes.

✓ Firstly, it's the "Breath Break." Take a minute to simply breathe, and give yourself a pause before responding—trust me, it's a game-changer.

✓ Next up, we have the "Perspective Shift." Sometimes, hardship appears overwhelming, yet a minor adjustment in perspective may convert a mountain into a molehill.

✓ Then there's the "Solution Focus." Instead of concentrating on the issue, divert that energy toward discovering solutions. It's about being proactive, not reactive.

✓ And let's not forget the "Support Connection." Reach out to friends, relatives, or a support network. Sometimes, sharing the weight makes things lighter.

These methods aren't about evading misfortune; they're about negotiating it with a brave poise.

So, join me in examining these practical tactics to keep cool-headed amid the heat of life's trials. Composure isn't simply a quality; it's a gift, and we can develop it together.

Conclusion

- Summarizing the 7 Principles

To summarize:

✓ Concentrate efforts solely on what is within your power to affect directly to prevent aggravation over the unpredictable.

✓ *Harness the power of rationality and clear thinking to conquer toxic emotions;* Navigate emotions with reason; perceive them as possibilities for insight and progress rather than succumbing to negative responses.

✓ *Welcome adversities as training grounds to cultivate self-discipline over time*; Transform failures into stepping stones; view obstacles as opportunities for personal growth and resilience.

✓ *Reflect on death regularly to encourage intentional behavior in the present;* Embrace the transience of existence; ponder on life's impermanence to prioritize some acts and cherish the current moment.

✓ Cultivate a thankful mentality; achieve satisfaction by appreciating what you have, changing attention from scarcity to plenty.

✓ Align with the natural order; understand what's within your control, accept the rest, and adjust with resilience.

✓ Build mental fortitude; accept adversities with equanimity, perceiving them as chances for character growth.

These ideas create the Stoic toolbox, giving a roadmap to living with knowledge, resilience, and calmness in life's uncertainties.

- Encouraging Continued Practice and Growth

As we conclude these seven Stoic concepts, it's essential I outline the significance of continual practice and progress. Stoicism isn't a one-time remedy; it's a lifetime path of self-discovery and personal improvement.

✓ ***Consistent Practice:*** - Embrace these ideals as everyday companions. Regularly review and use them, converting them from ideas into habits. Consistency is the key to internalizing Stoic knowledge.

✓ ***Learn from obstacles:*** - Life is a perpetual teacher, and obstacles are lessons. Approach problems with a Stoic perspective, seeing them not as hurdles but as chances for progress. Each attempt is an opportunity to enhance your knowledge and implement these ideas.

✓ ***Cultivate a Growth mentality:*** - Adopt a growth mentality that thrives on learning and resilience. Stoicism urges us to regard setbacks as stepping stones, failures as lessons, and the journey itself as a continuous process.

✓ ***Seek Community and Support:*** - Connect with like-minded others on a similar Stoic path. Share experiences, problems, and successes. A supportive group may give significant insights and encouragement during periods of development.

✓ ***Adapt and Refine:*** - Life is dynamic, and so should be your practice of Stoicism. Be open to altering and improving your knowledge of these ideas as you traverse the ever-changing landscapes of your own path.

In conclusion, Stoicism is not a destination but a route—a path towards increased self-awareness, resilience, and peace.

Enjoy your journey, remain devoted to your improvement, and allow these Stoic ideas to be your guiding lights in the search for a more meaningful and fulfilled existence.